FOR ORGANS, PIANOS & ELECTRONIC KEYBOARDS

E-Z PLAY TODAY
154

walk the line
MUSIC FROM THE MOTION PICTURE SOUNDTRACK

T0087647

FOX 2000 PICTURES PRESENTS A TREE/LINE FILM PRODUCTION AND A CATFISH PRODUCTION A FILM BY JAMES MANGOLD

JOAQUIN PHOENIX REESE WITHERSPOON "WALK THE LINE" GINNIFER GOODWIN ROBERT PATRICK

MUSIC BY T BONE BURNETT EXECUTIVE MUSIC PRODUCER T BONE BURNETT COSTUME DESIGNER ARIANNE PHILLIPS FILM EDITOR MICHAEL McCUSKER PRODUCTION DESIGNER DAVID J. BOMBA

DIRECTOR OF PHOTOGRAPHY PHEDON PAPAMICHAEL, ASC EXECUTIVE PRODUCERS JOHN CARTER CASH ALAN C. BLOMQUIST PRODUCED BY CATHY KONRAD AND JAMES KEACH

BASED ON "MAN IN BLACK" AND "CASH THE AUTOBIOGRAPHY", WRITTEN BY JOHNNY CASH WRITTEN BY GILL DENNIS & JAMES MANGOLD DIRECTED BY JAMES MANGOLD

20th CENTURY FOX

ORIGINAL CAST ALBUM AVAILABLE ON WIND-UP RECORDS   www.walkthelinethemovie.com   DOLBY IN SELECTED THEATRES   ©2005 Twentieth Century Fox

ISBN-13: 978-1-4234-2116-0
ISBN-10: 1-4234-2116-7

HAL•LEONARD® CORPORATION
7777 W. BLUEMOUND RD. P.O. BOX 13819 MILWAUKEE, WI 53213

Visit Hal Leonard Online at
www.halleonard.com

contents

Get Rhythm

Registration 8
Rhythm: Country or Fox Trot

Words and Music by
John R. Cash

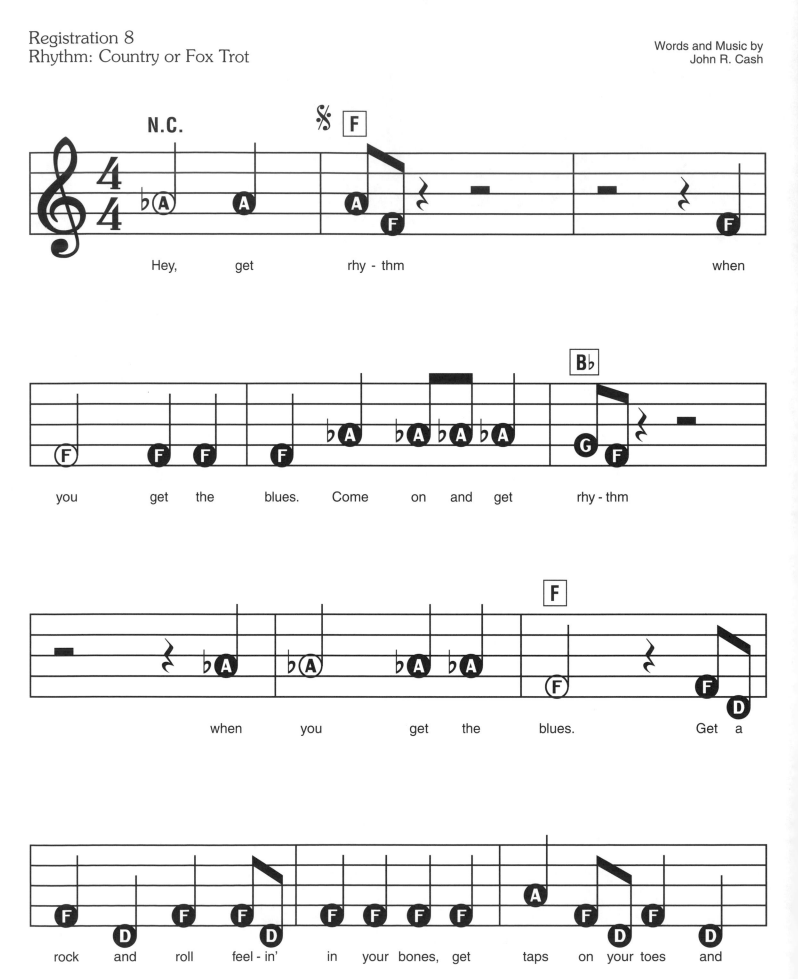

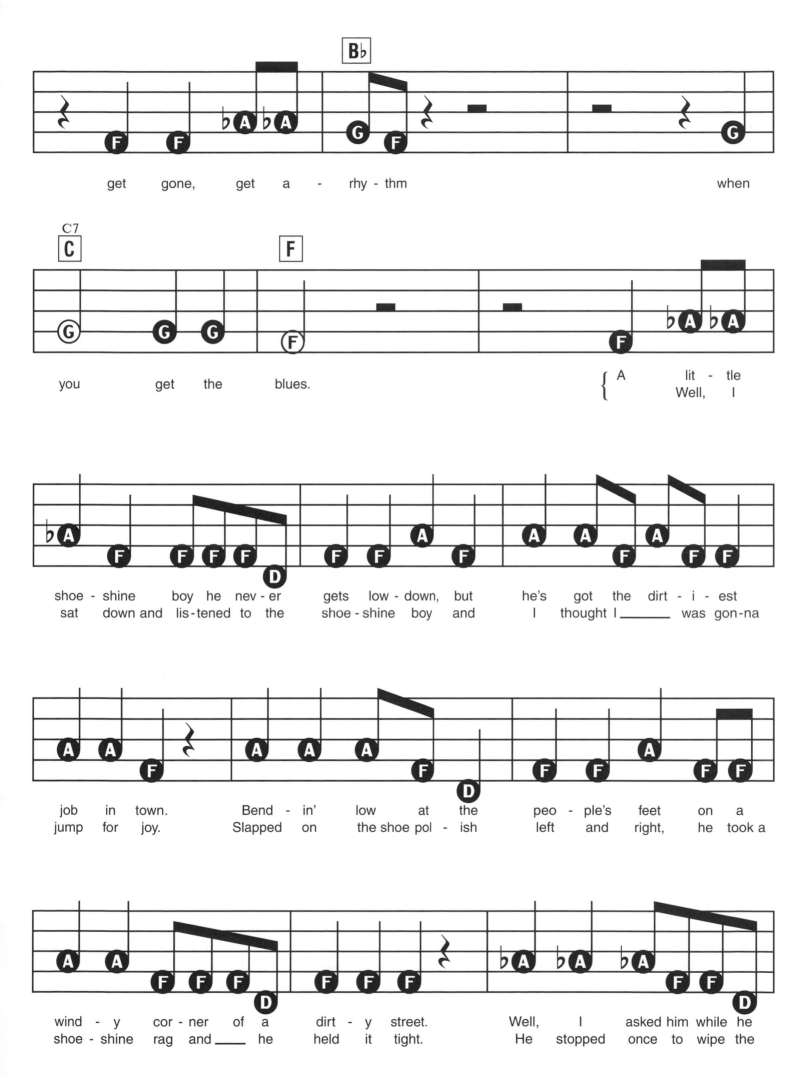

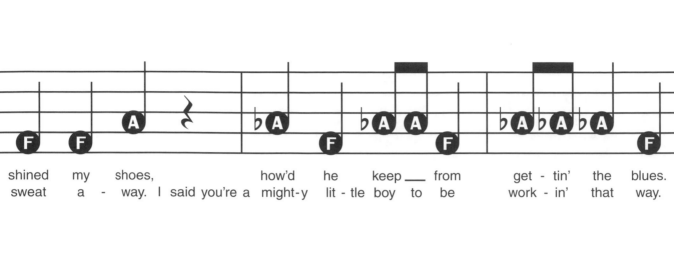

shined my shoes, how'd he keep ___ from get - tin' the blues. He
sweat a - way. I said you're a might-y lit - tle boy to be work - in' that way. He

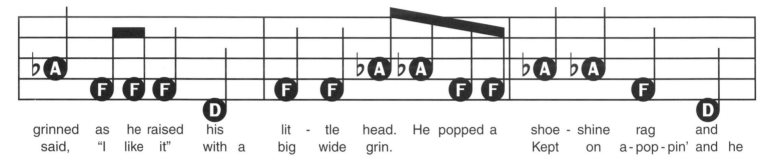

grinned as he raised his lit - tle head. He popped a shoe - shine rag and
said, "I like it" with a big wide grin. Kept on a - pop-pin' and he

then he said } get rhy - thm
said a - gain } when

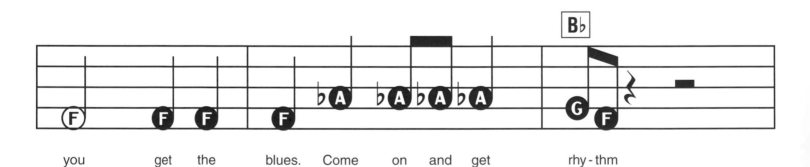

B♭

you get the blues. Come on and get rhy - thm

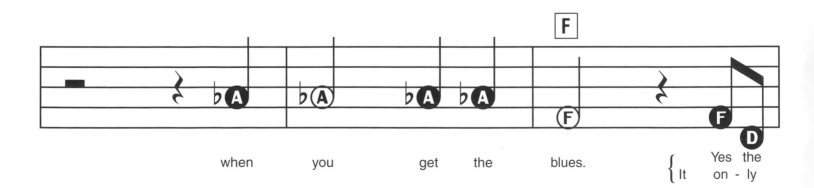

F

when you get the blues. { Yes the
{ It on - ly

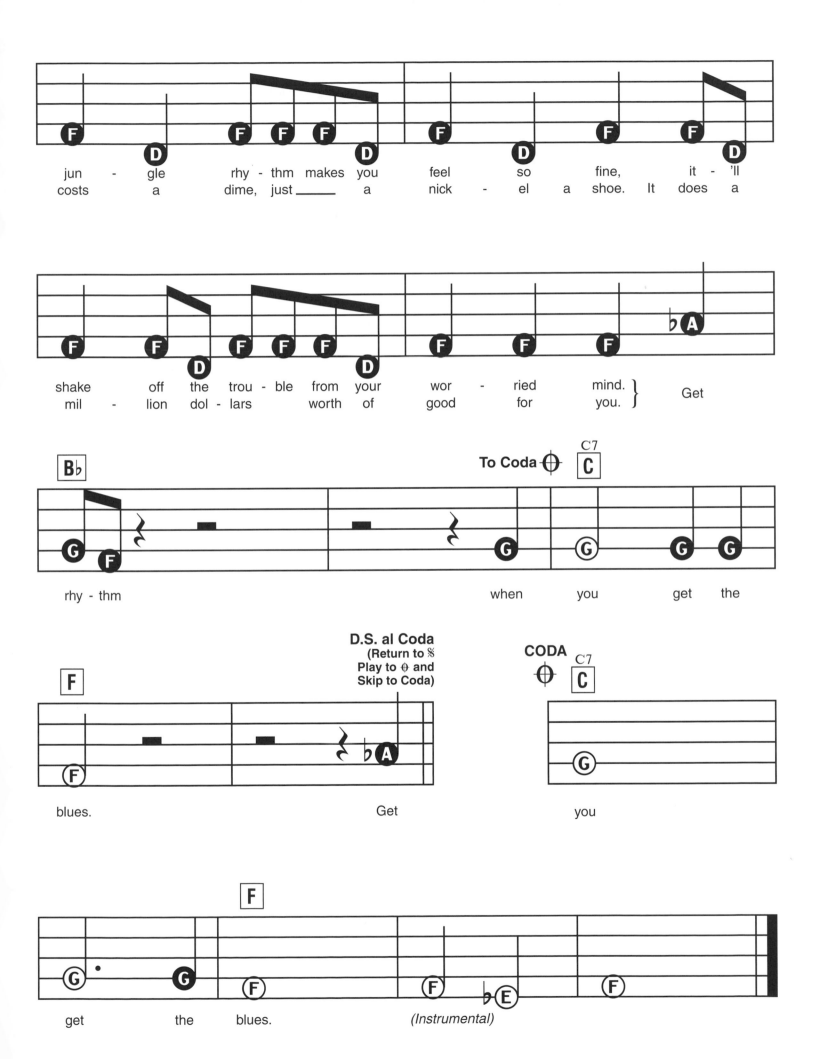

I Walk the Line

Registration 8
Rhythm: Country or Ballad

Words and Music by
John R. Cash

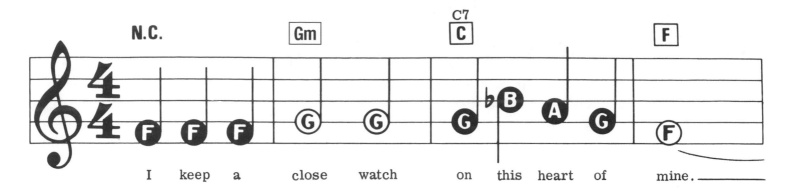

I keep a close watch on this heart of mine.

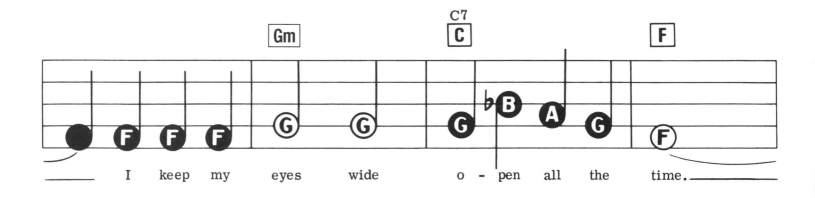

I keep my eyes wide o - pen all the time.

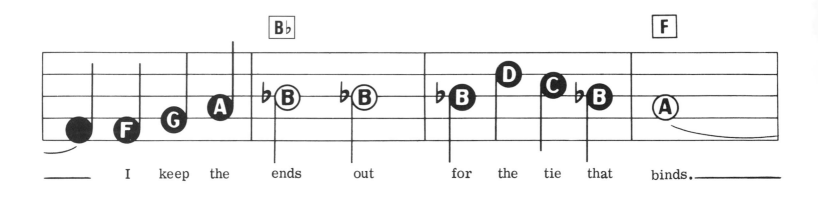

I keep the ends out for the tie that binds.

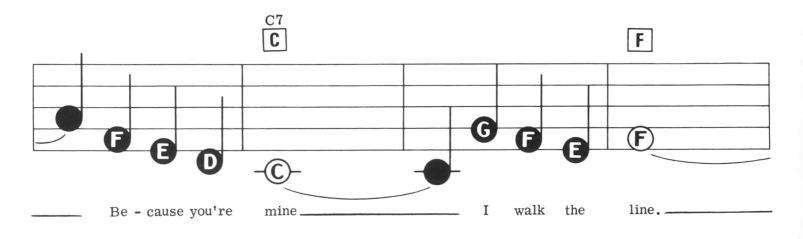

Be - cause you're mine I walk the line.

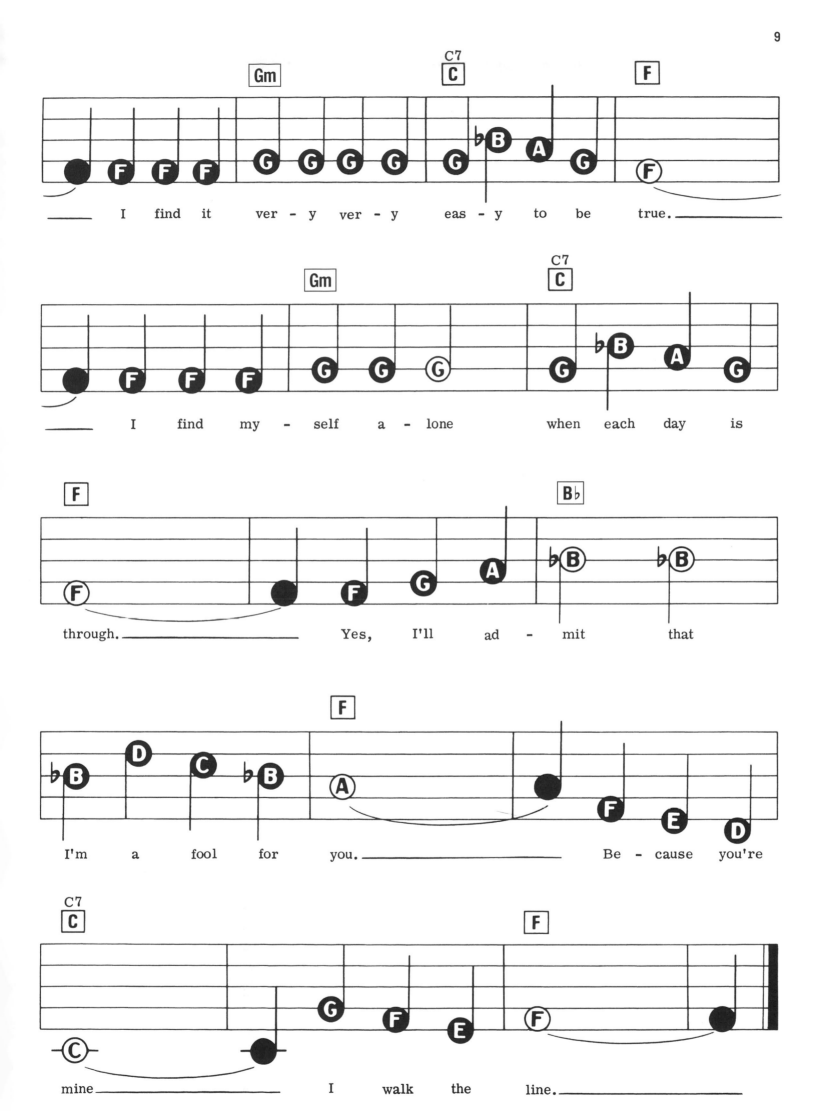

Wildwood Flower

Registration 4
Rhythm: Country or Fox Trot

Words and Music by
A.P. Carter

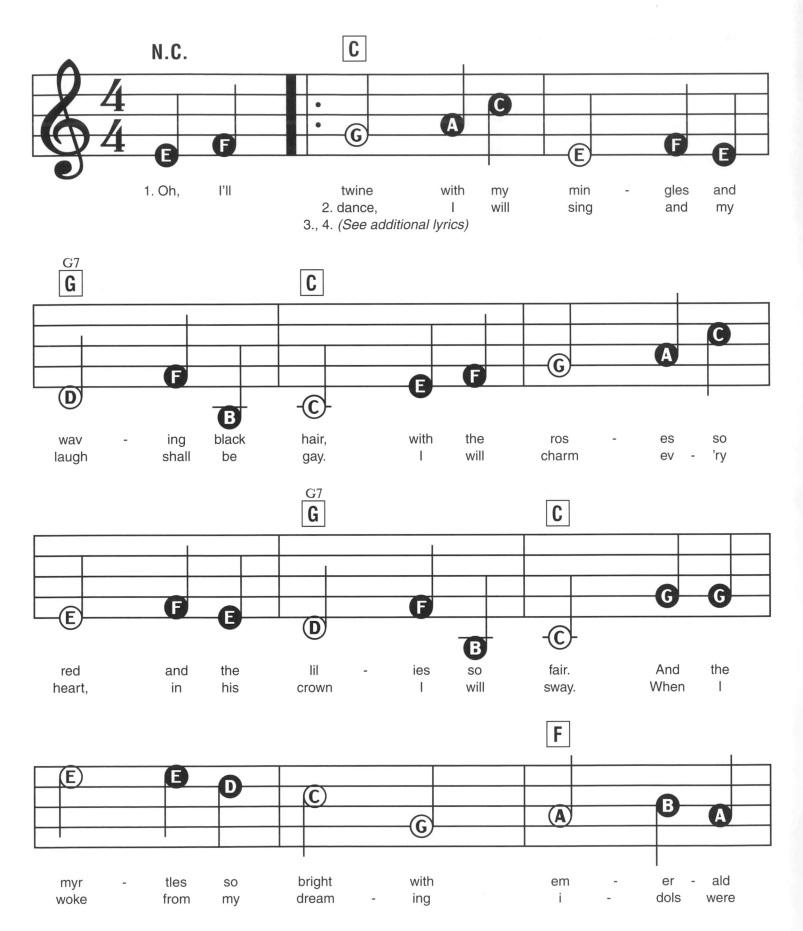

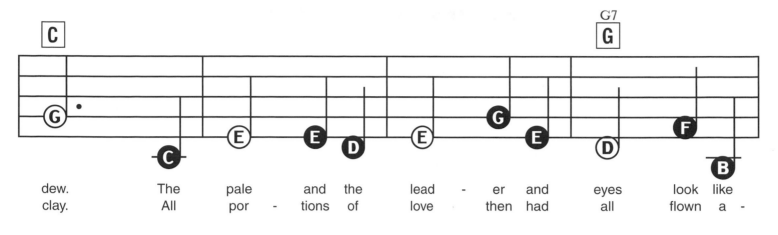

dew.   The   pale   and   the   lead   -   er   and   eyes   look   like

clay.   All   por -   tions   of   love   then   had   all   flown   a -

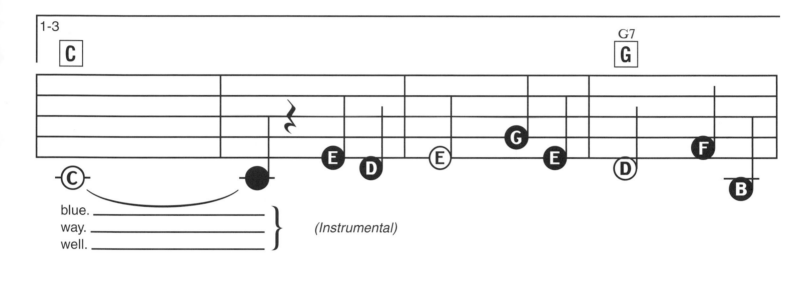

blue. _____

way. _____ } *(Instrumental)*

well. _____

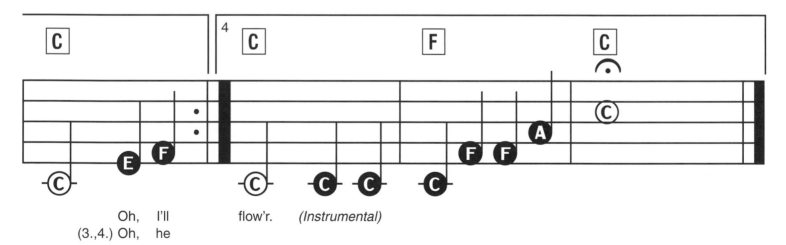

Oh,   I'll   flow'r.   *(Instrumental)*

(3.,4.) Oh,   he

Additional Lyrics

3. Oh, he taught me to love him and promised to love,
   And to cherish me over all others above.
   How my heart now is wond'ring misery can tell.
   He's left me no warning, no words of farewell.

4. Oh, he taught me to love him and called me his flow'r,
   That was blooming to cheer him through life's dreary hour.
   Oh, I'm longing to see him through life's dark hour.
   He's gone and neglected this pale wildwood flow'r.

Ring of Fire

Registration 3
Rhythm: Rock

Words and Music by Merle Kilgore
and June Carter

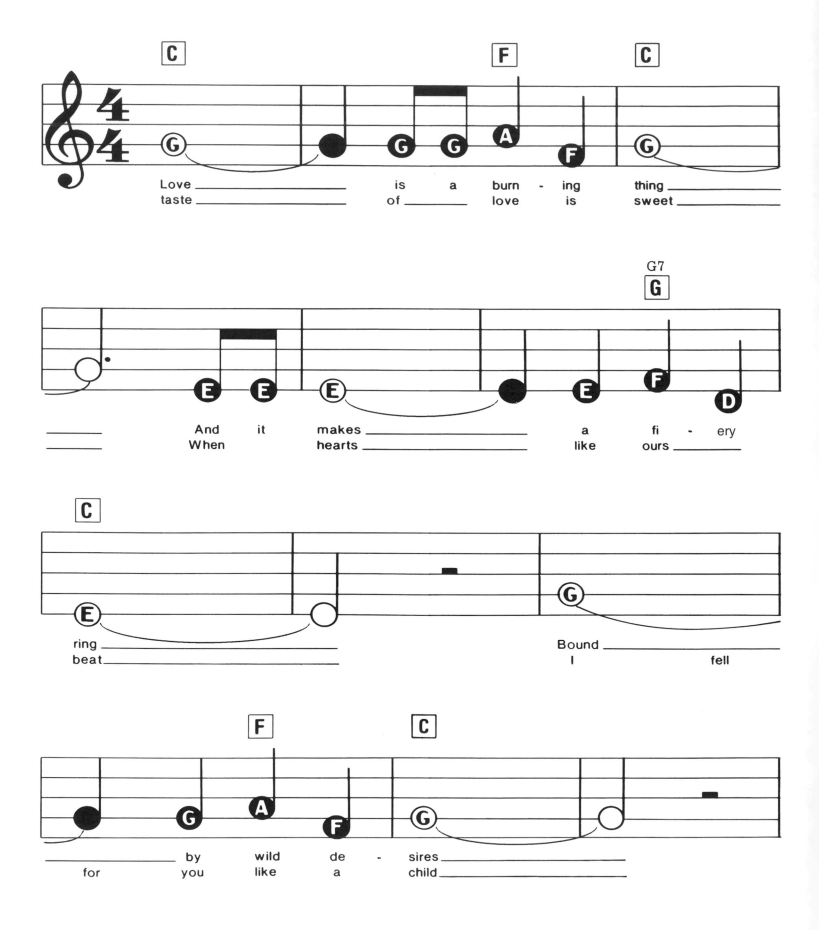

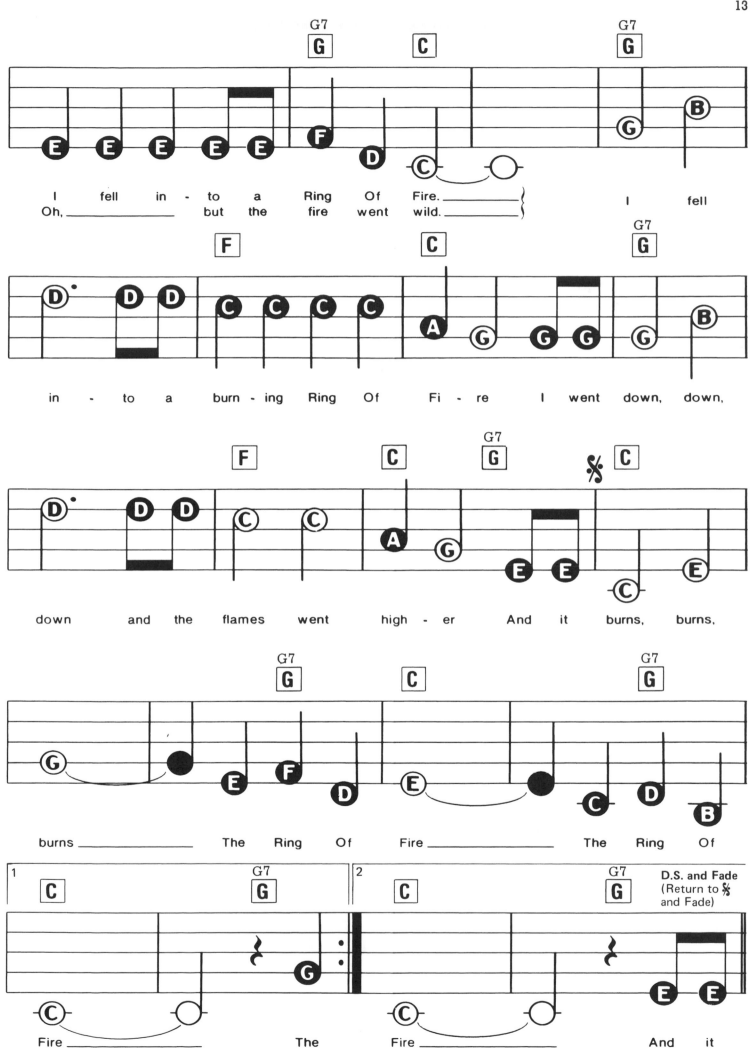

You're My Baby

Registration 2
Rhythm: Bluegrass or Fox Trot

Words and Music by
John R. Cash

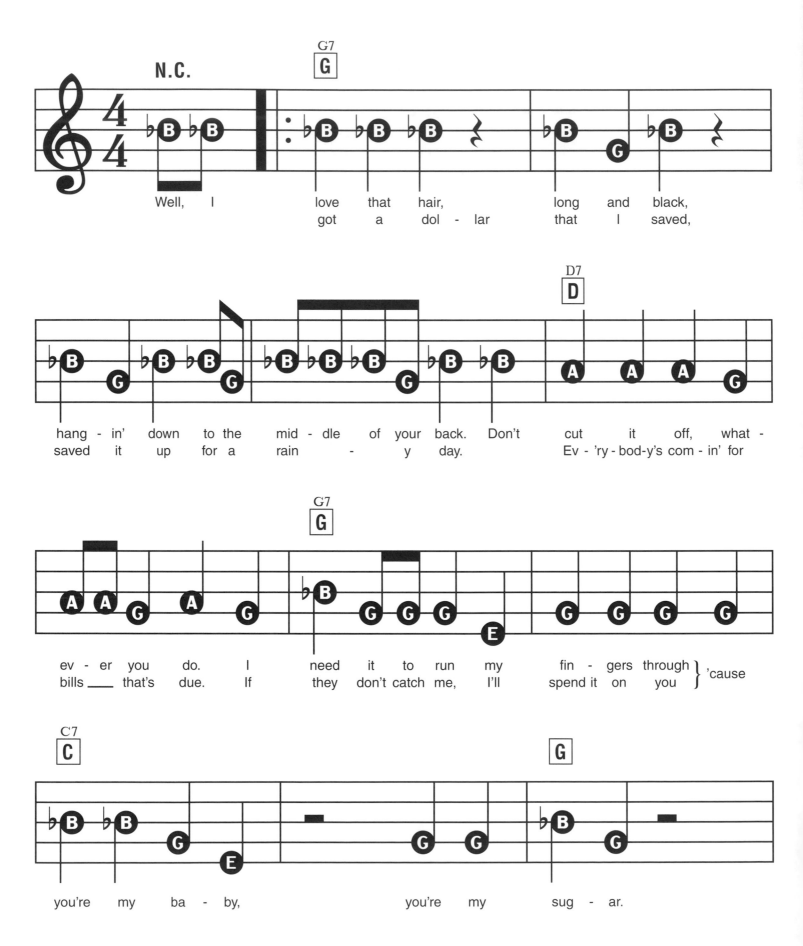

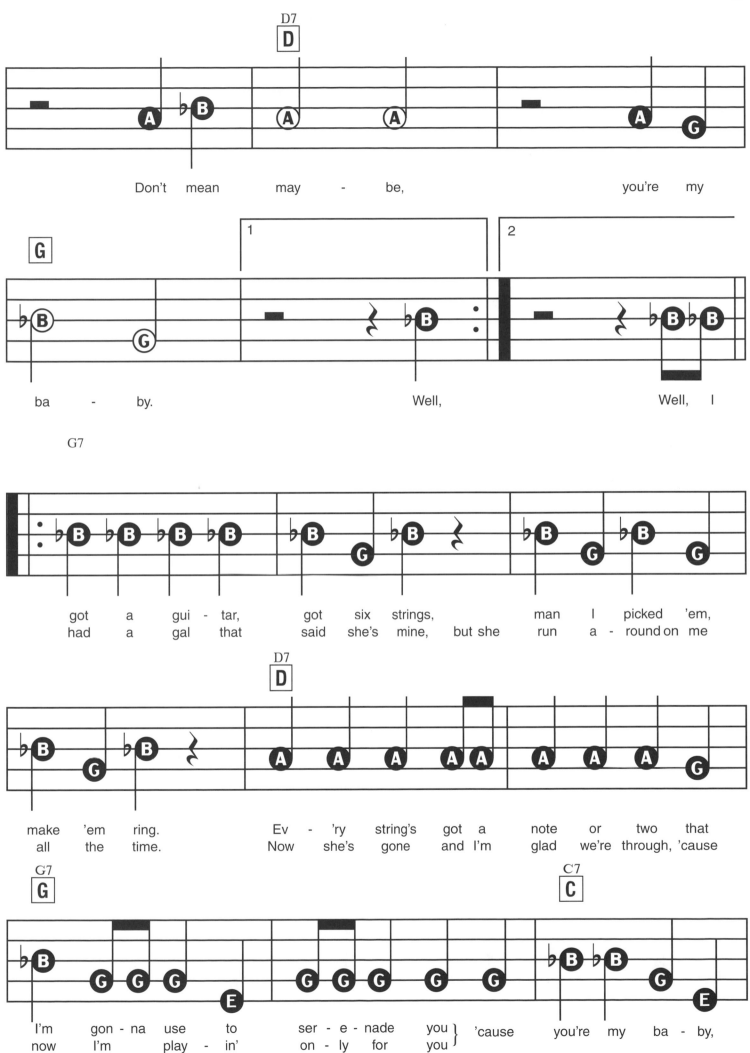

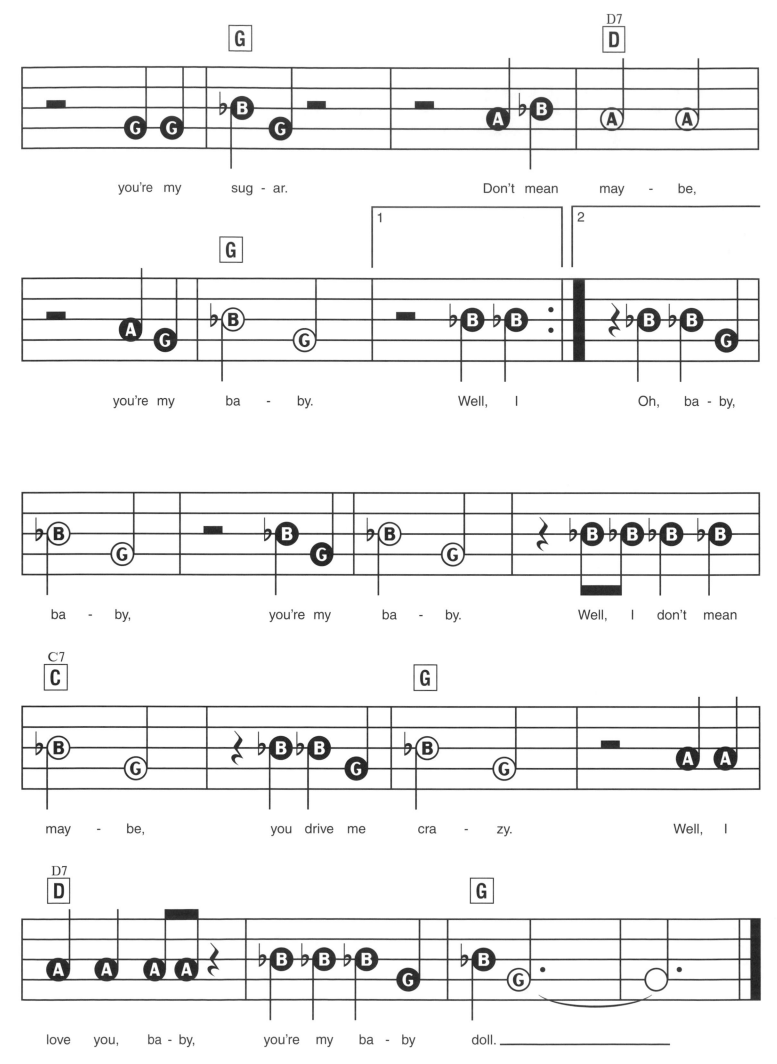

Cry, Cry, Cry

Registration 1
Rhythm: Country or Fox Trot

Words and Music by
John R. Cash

N.C. **F**

G G A G | A A G | A A G

Ev - 'ry - bod - y   knows   where   you   go   when   the

A F | F G | A G A G | A F F F

sun   goes   down.   I   think   you   on - ly   live   to   see   the

G7 **G**   **C7** **C**   **F**

G G | G G | A A G A G A G

lights   up - town.   I   wast - ed   my   time   when   I   would

Bb

A F | F F | D F F F

try,   try,   try,   'cause   when   the   lights   have

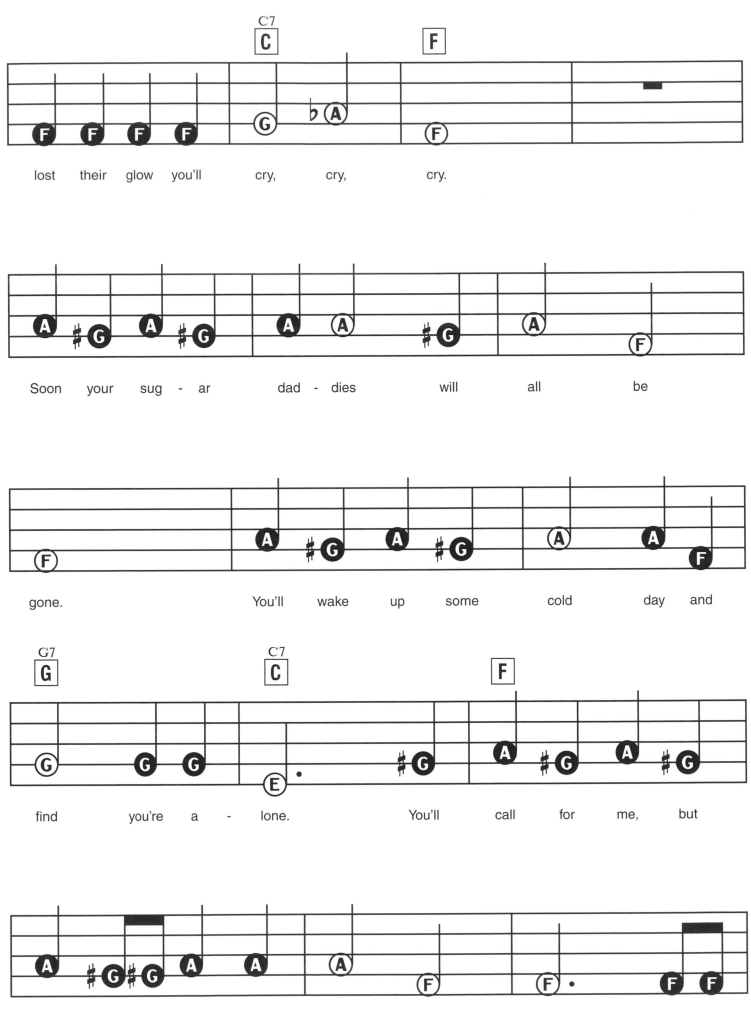

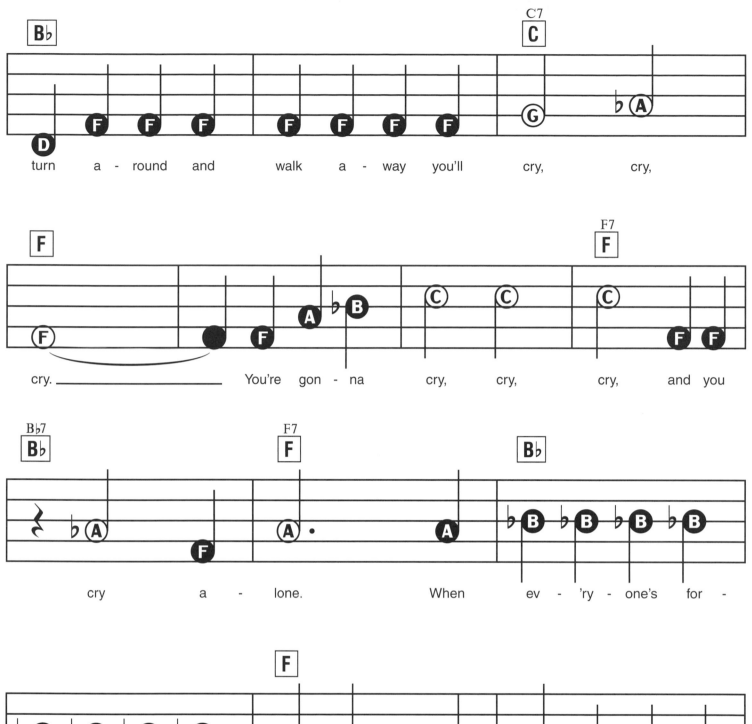

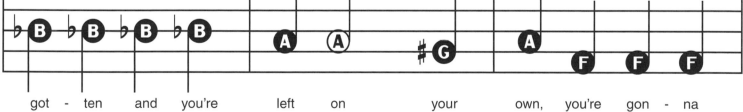

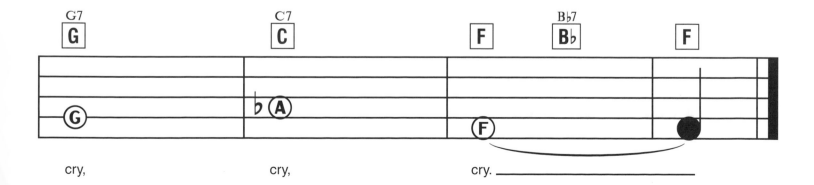

Folsom Prison Blues

Registration 3
Rhythm: Rock or Fox Trot

Words and Music by
John R. Cash

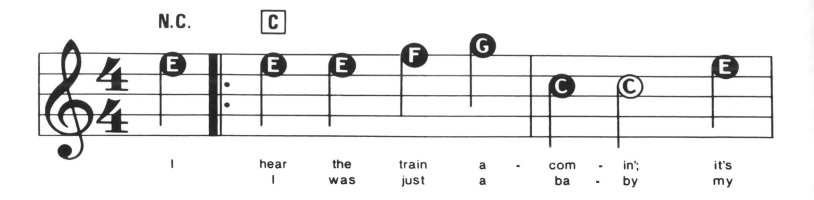

I hear the train a - com - in'; it's
I was just a ba - by my

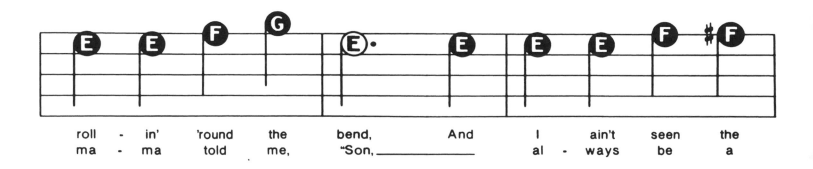

roll - in' 'round the bend, And I ain't seen the
ma - ma told me, "Son,_____ al - ways be a

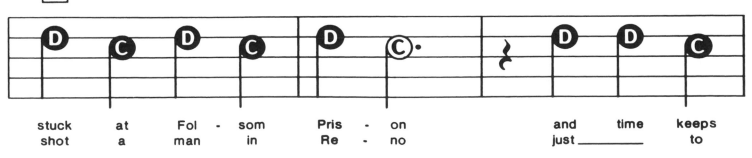

sun - shine since I don't know when. I'm
good boy; don't ever play with guns. But I

stuck at Fol - som Pris - on and time keeps
shot a man in Re - no just_____ to

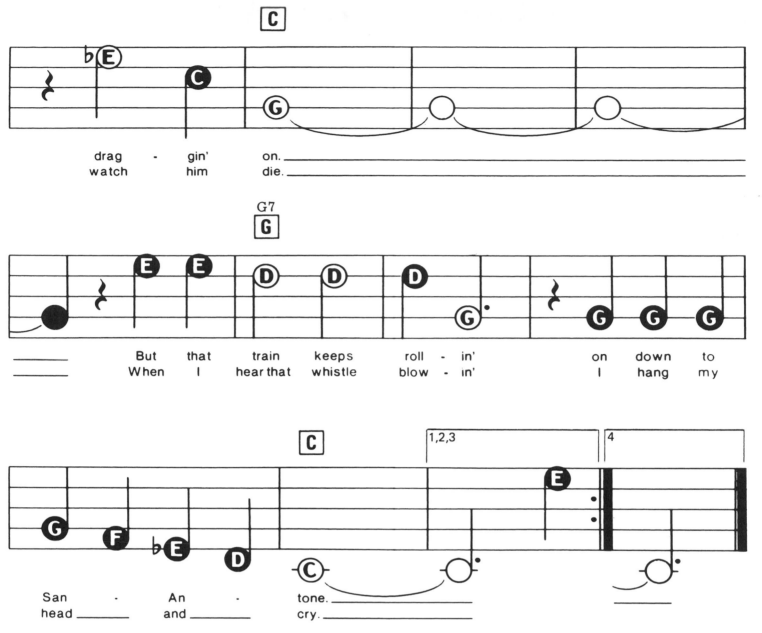

3. I bet there's rich folks eatin' in a fancy dining car.
   They're prob'ly drinkin' coffee and smokin' big cigars,
   But I know I had it comin', I know I can't be free,
   But those people keep a-movin', and that's what tortures me.

4. Well, if they freed me from this prison, if that railroad train was mine,
   I bet I'd move over a little farther down the line,
   Far from Folsom Prison, that's where I want to stay.
   And I'd let that lonesome whistle blow my blues away.

That's All Right

Registration 4
Rhythm: Rock

Words and Music by
Arthur Crudup

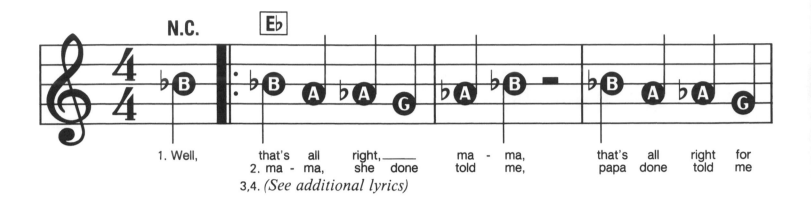

1. Well, that's all right,_____ ma - ma, that's all right for
2. ma - ma, she done told me, papa done right told me

3,4. *(See additional lyrics)*

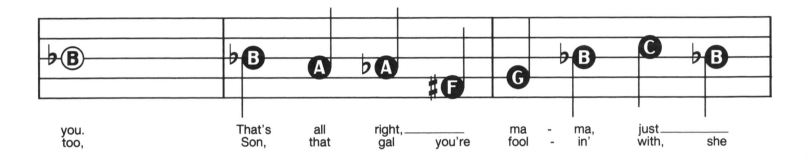

you. That's all right,_____ ma - ma, just_____
too, Son, that right gal you're fool - in' with, she

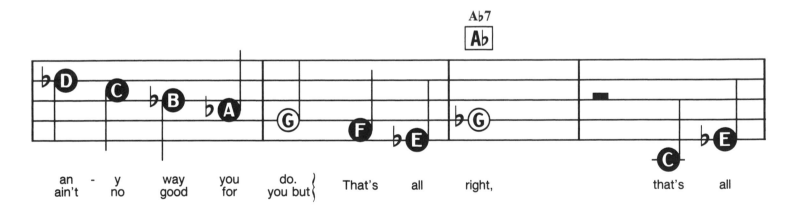

an - y way you do. That's all right, that's all
ain't no good for you but you.

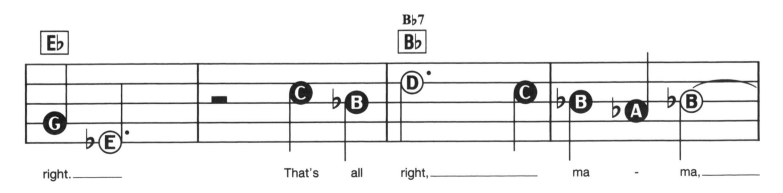

right._____ That's all right,_____ ma - ma,

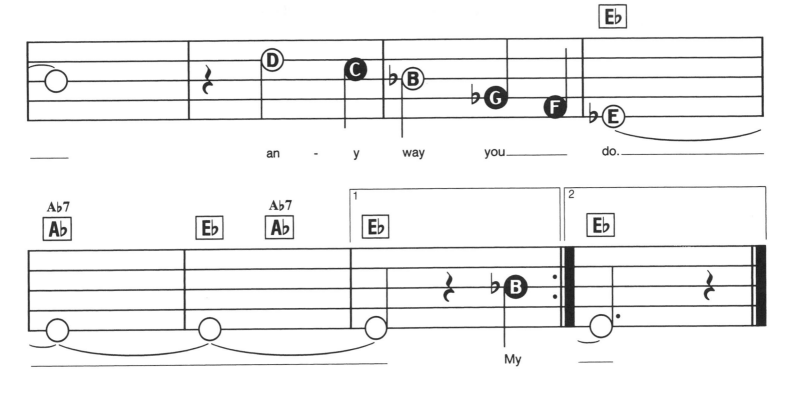

Additional Lyrics

3. I'm leavin' town tomorrow, leavin' town for sure,
Then you won't be bothered with me hangin' 'round your door,
But that's all right, that's all right.
That's all right, mama, any way you do.

4. I oughta mind my papa, guess I'm not too smart.
If I was I'd leave you, go before you break my heart,
But that's all right, that's all right.
That's all right, mama, any way you do.

Juke Box Blues

Registration 8
Rhythm: Country Pop or Fox Trot

Words and Music by Helen Carter
and Maybelle Carter

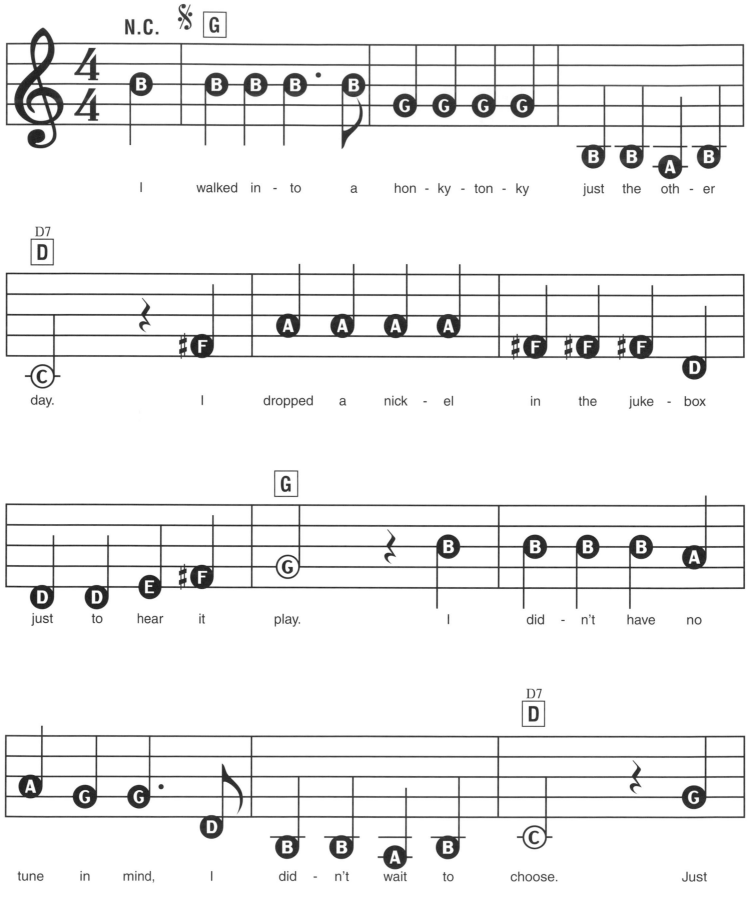

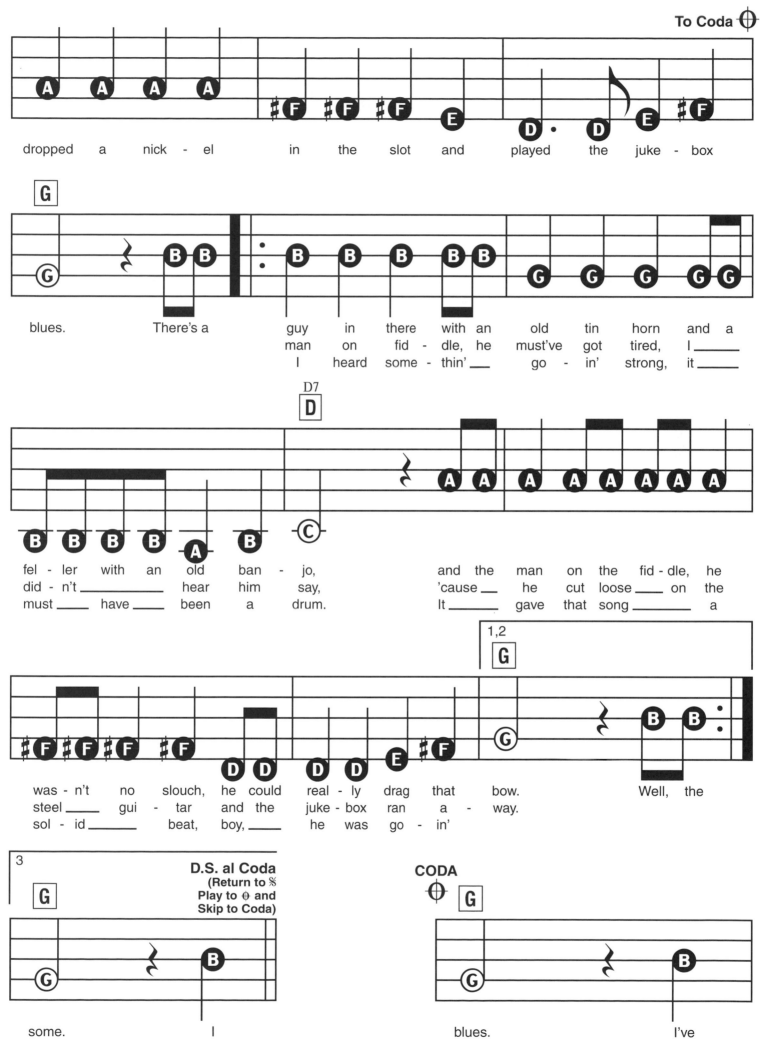

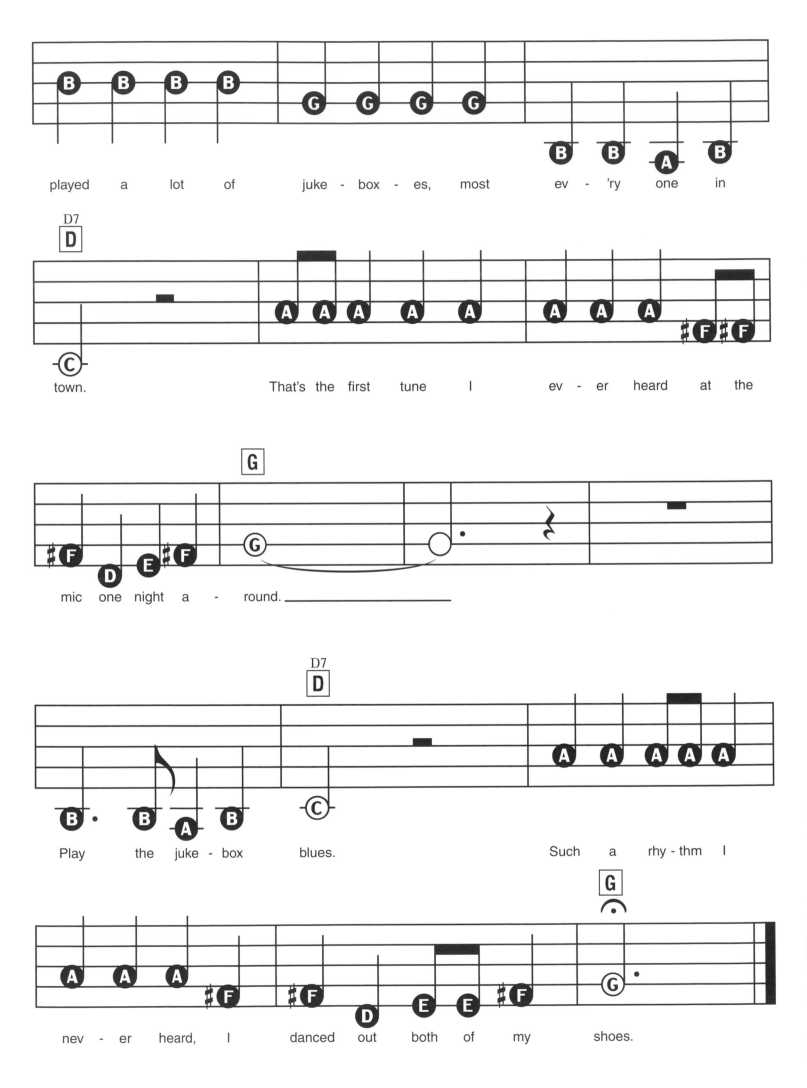

It Ain't Me, Babe

Registration 4
Rhythm: Country Pop or Fox Trot

Words and Music by
Bob Dylan

C

E E E   E   G   **Dm** E D·

Go a - way   from my win - dow,
light - ly   from the ledge, babe,

C   **G**   **C**

E E G E E D C

leave at your own cho - sen speed.
go light - ly _____ on the _____ ground.

Dm

D E E E G E D

I'm not the one you want, babe.
I'm not the one you want, babe.

C   **G**   **C**

D E· G E D C

I'm not the one you need.
I'll on - ly let you down.

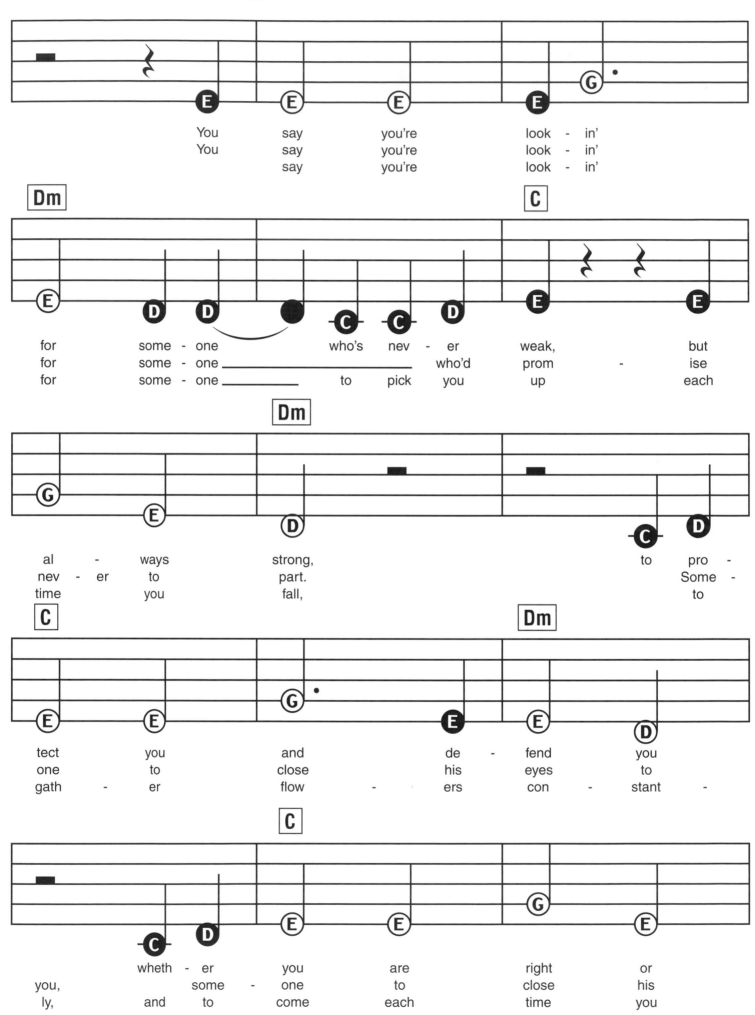

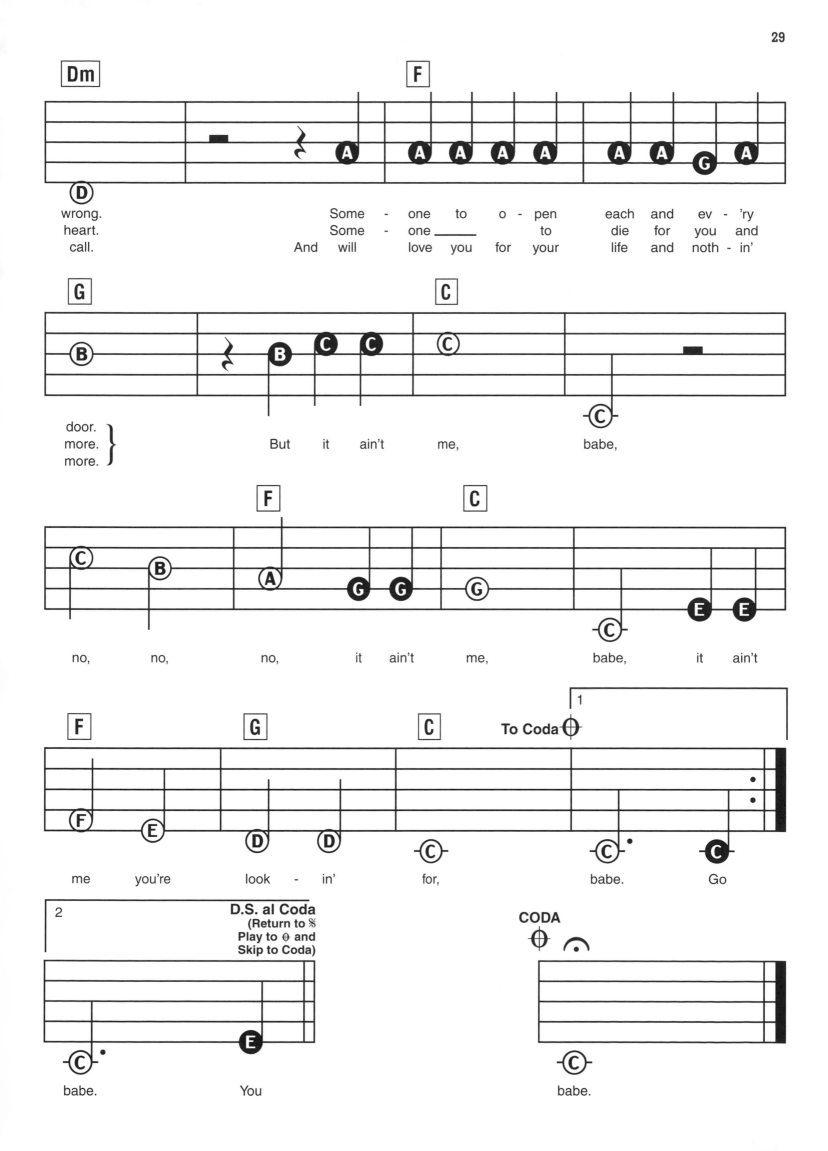

Home of the Blues

Registration 4
Rhythm: Bluegrass or Fox Trot

Written by John R. Cash,
Lillie McAlpin and Glenn Douglas

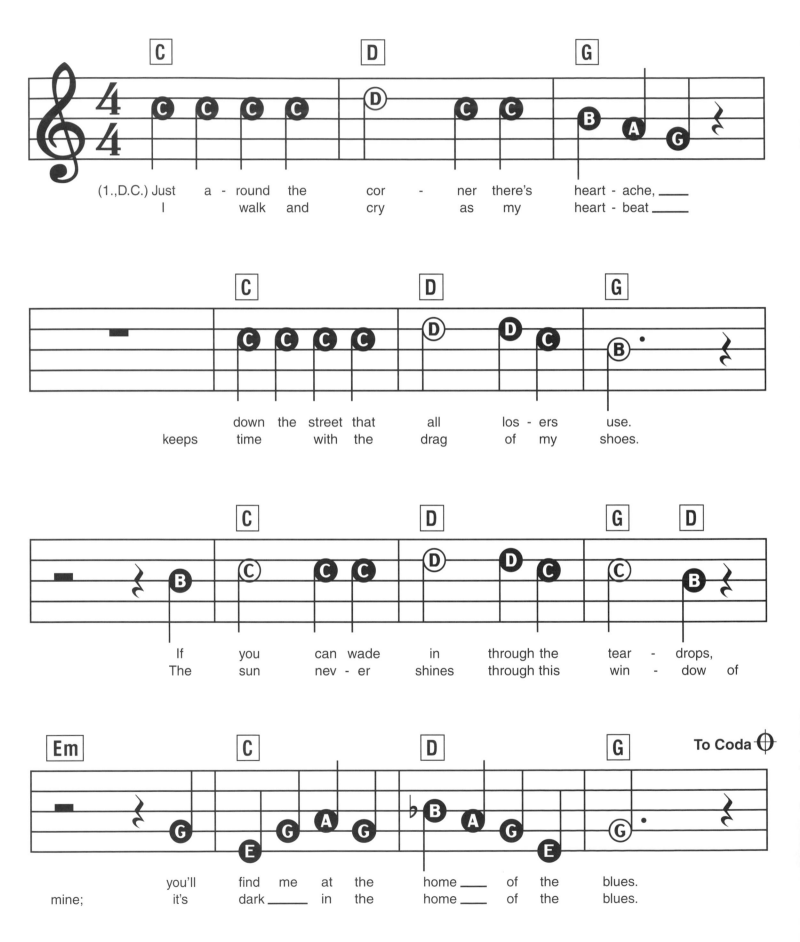

31

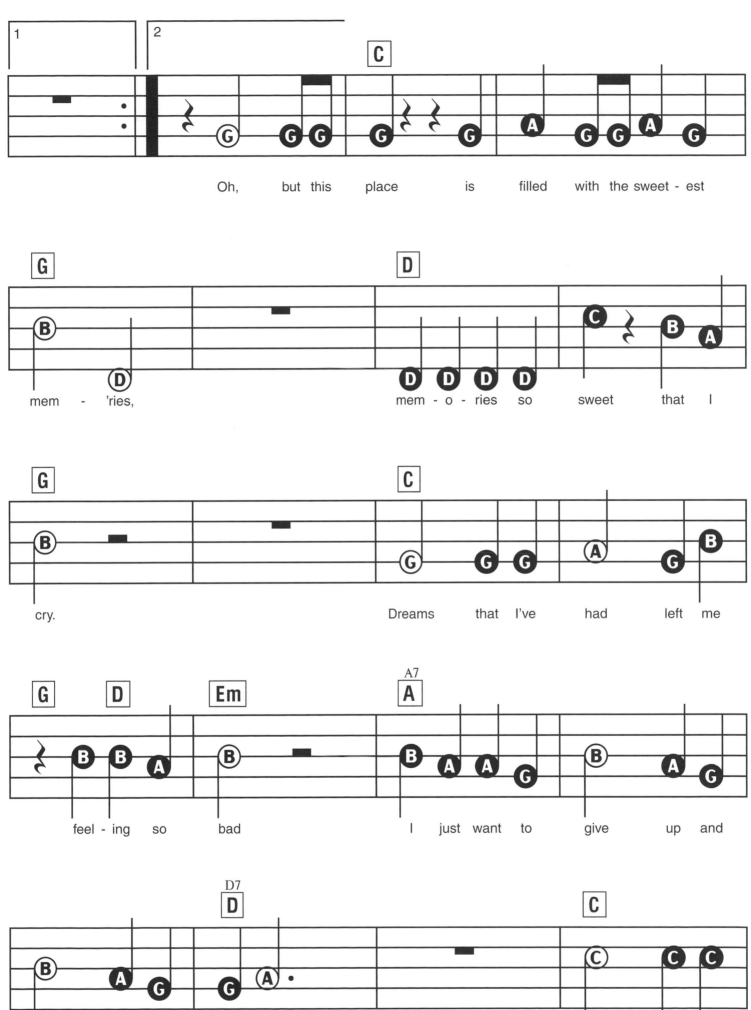

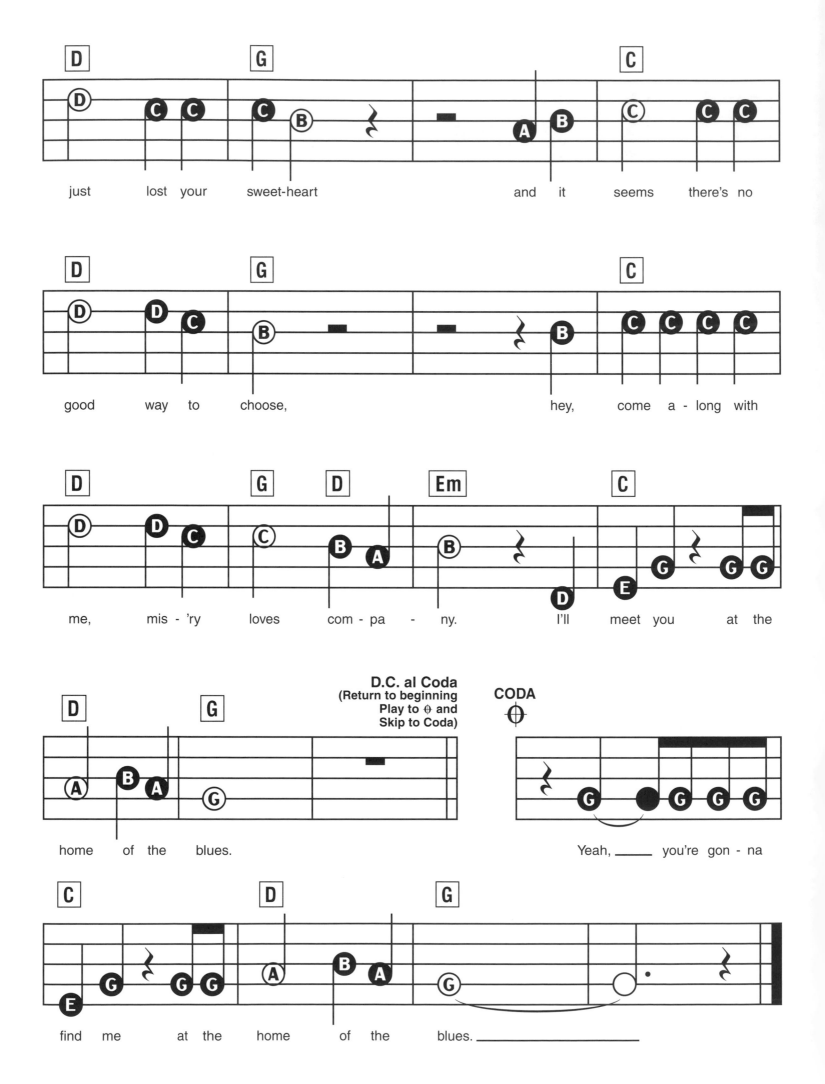

Cocaine Blues

Registration 8
Rhythm: Country Pop or Fox Trot

Words and Music by
T.J. Arnall

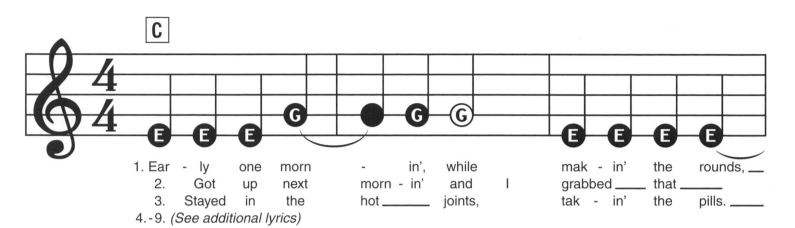

1. Ear - ly one morn - in', while mak - in' the rounds, __
2. Got up next morn - in' and I grabbed ___ that ___
3. Stayed in the hot ___ joints, tak - in' the pills. __
4.-9. *(See additional lyrics)*

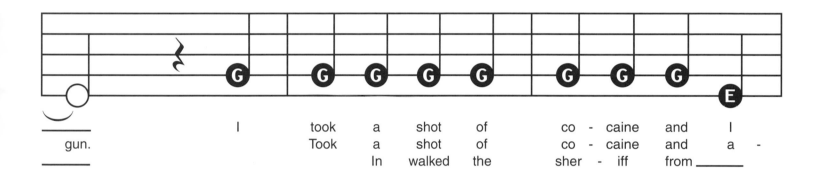

__ gun. I took a shot of co - caine and I
Took a shot of co - caine and a -
In walked the sher - iff from ___

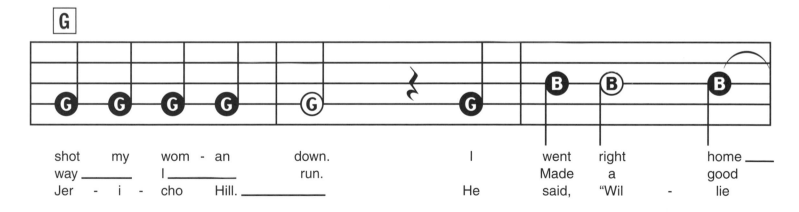

shot my wom - an down. I went right home __
way ___ I run. Made a good
Jer - i - cho Hill. ___ He said, "Wil - lie

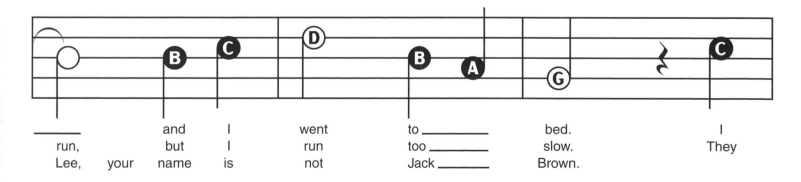

__ run, and I went to bed. I
run, but I run too ___ slow. They
Lee, your name is not Jack ___ Brown.

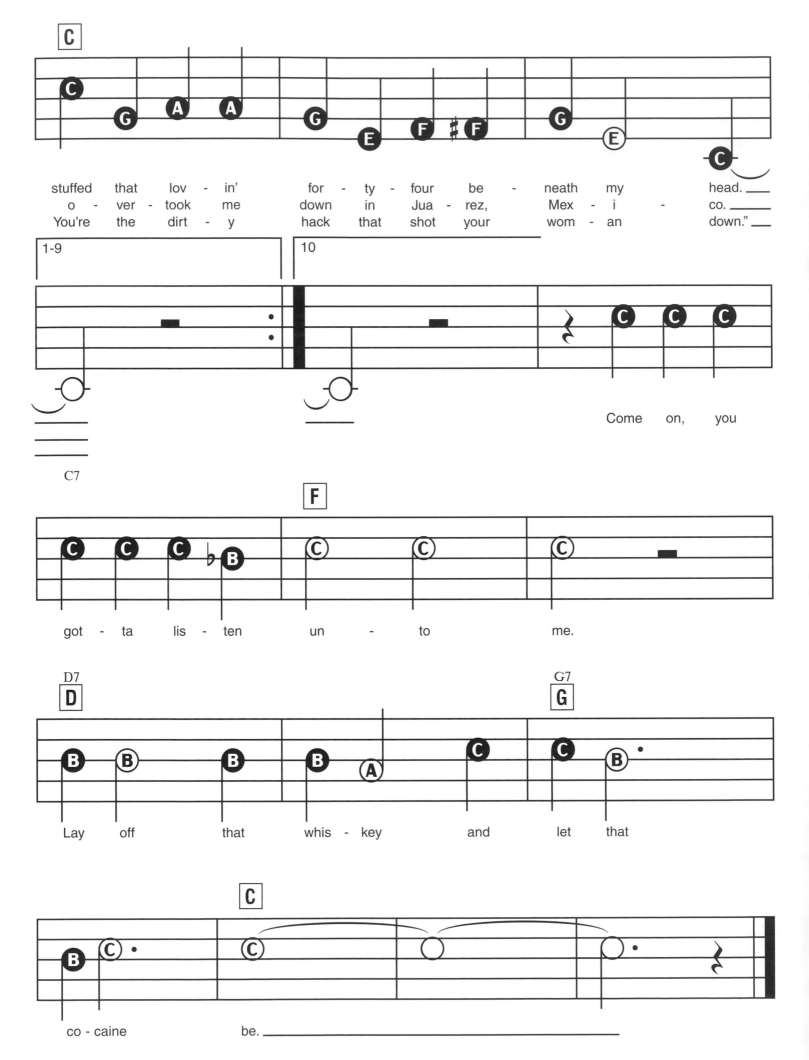

stuffed that lov - in'   for - ty - four   be - neath my   head. ___
o - ver - took   me   down in   Jua - rez,   Mex - i - co. ___
You're the dirt - y   hack that   shot your   wom - an   down." ___

1-9   10

C7

Come on, you

F

got - ta   lis - ten   un - to   me.

D7
D   G7
G

Lay   off   that   whis - key   and   let   that

C

co - caine   be. ___

Additional Lyrics

4. Hey, yes, oh yes, my name is Willie Lee.
   If you've got a warrant just read it to me.
   Shot her down because she made me sore.
   I thought I was her daddy, but she had five more.

5. When I was arrested, I was dressed in black.
   They put me on the train and they took me back.
   Had no friend for to go my bail,
   They slapped my dried-up carcass in the county jail.

6. Early the next mornin' about half-past nine
   I spot the sheriff comin' down the line.
   And he coughed as he cleared his throat,
   He said, "Come on, you dirty hack, into the district court."

7. Into the courtroom, my trial began,
   Where I was handled by twelve honest men.
   Just before the jury started out,
   I saw that little judge commence to look about.

8. Here in 'bout five minutes in walked the man,
   Holdin' the verdict in his right hand.
   The verdict read, "In the first degree."
   I hollered, "Lordy, Lordy, have mercy on me."

9. The judge, he smiled as he picked up his pen.
   Ninety-nine years in the Folsom pen.
   Ninety-nine years underneath the ground,
   I can't forget the day I shot that bad bitch down.

Milk Cow Blues

Registration 2
Rhythm: Blues or Country

Words and Music by
Kokomo Arnold

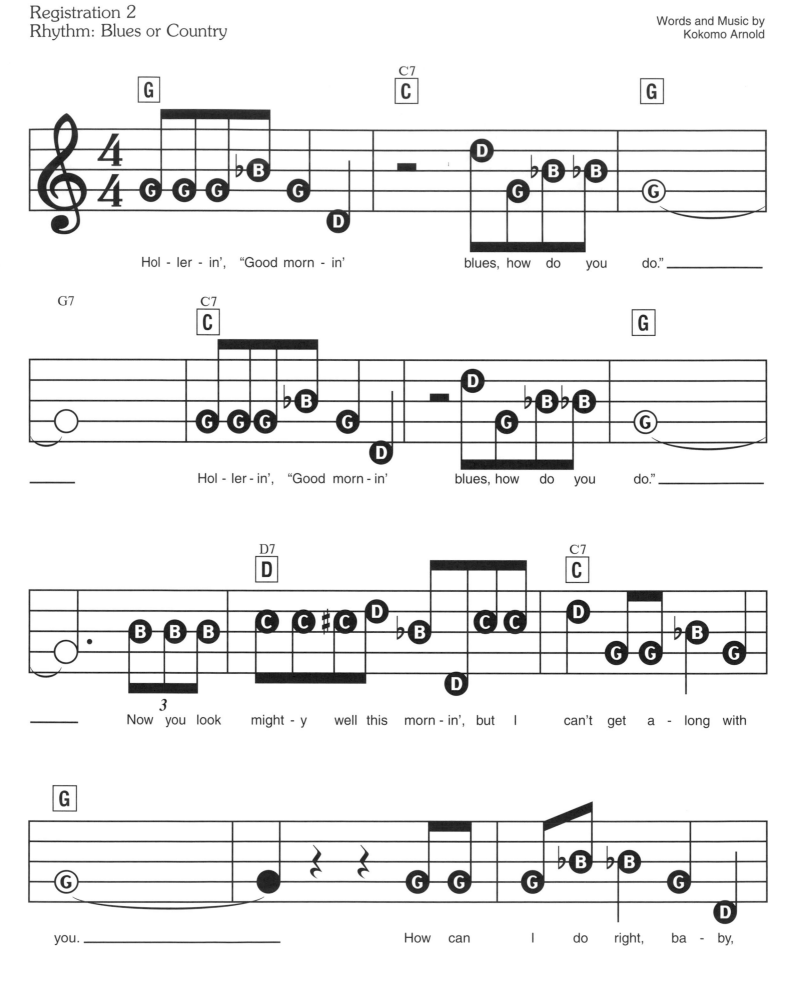

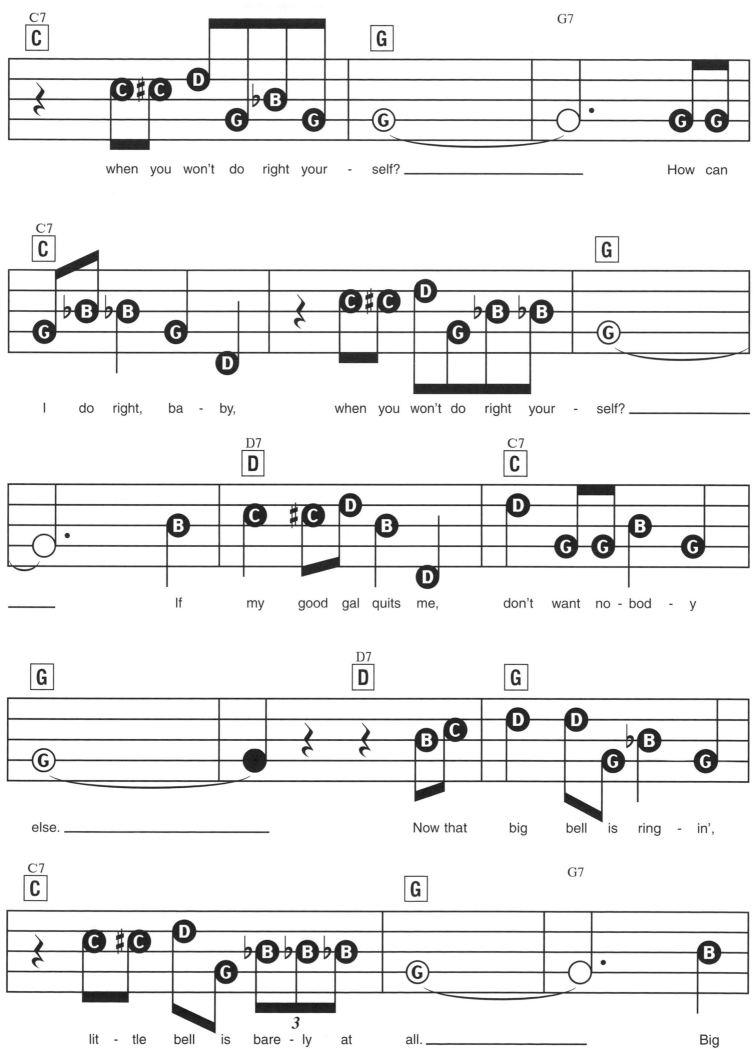

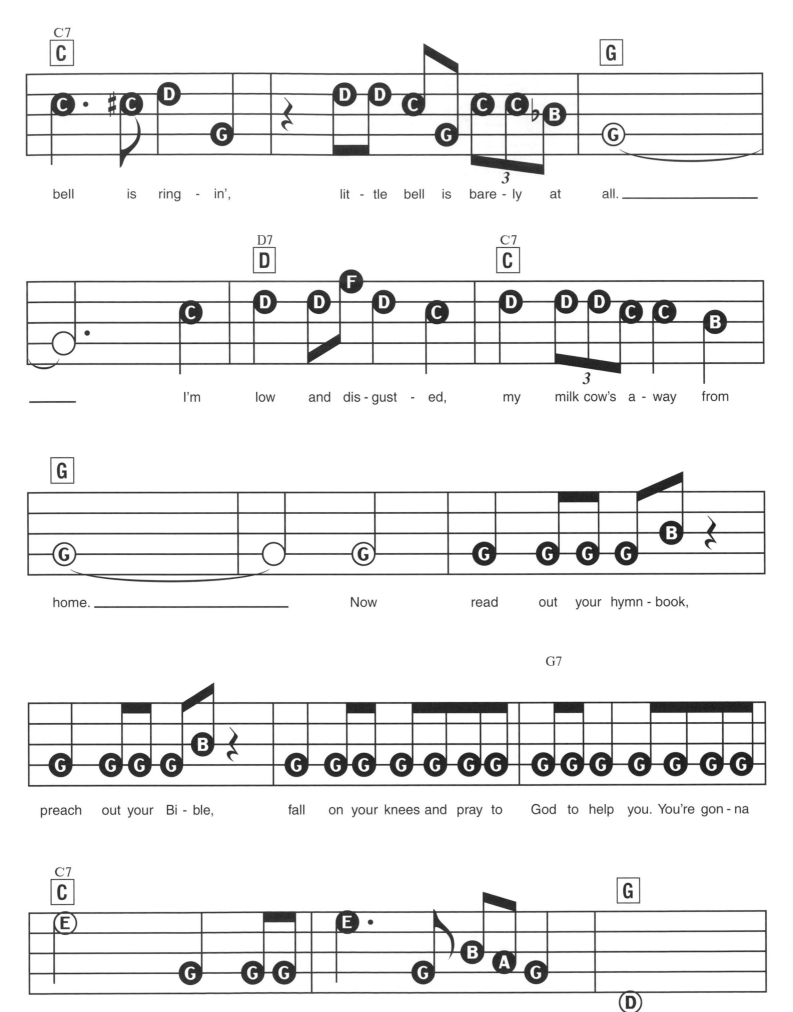

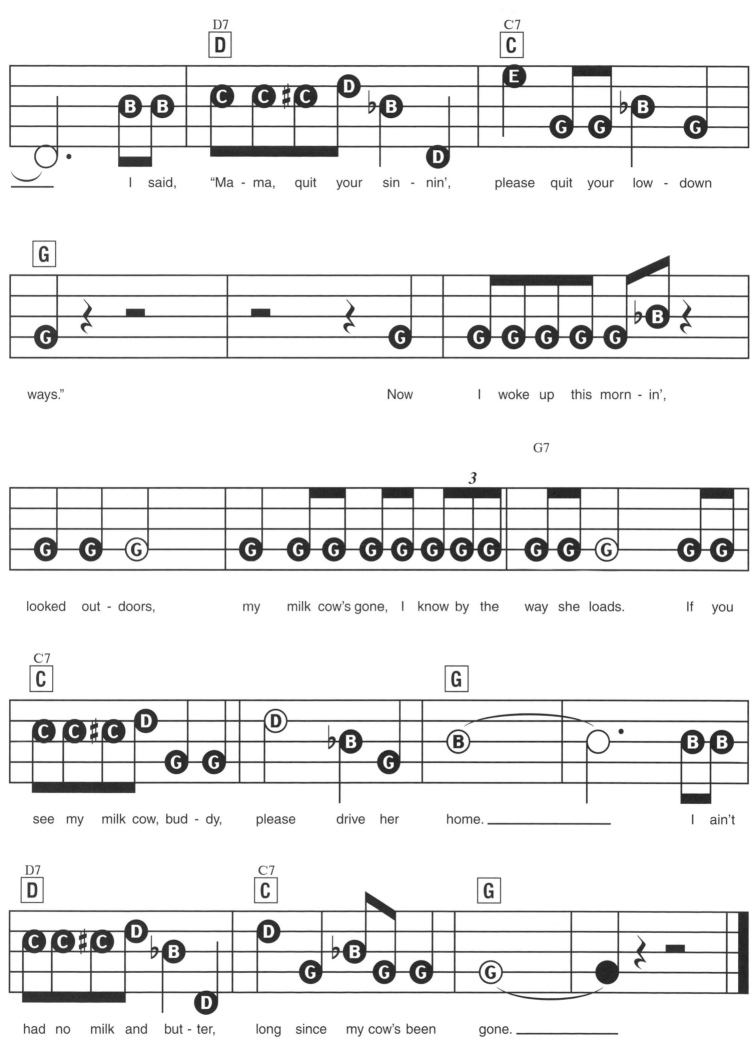

I'm a Long Way from Home

Registration 4
Rhythm: Country Swing or Country

Words and Music by
Hank Cochran

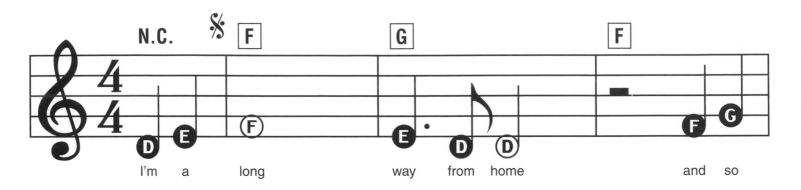

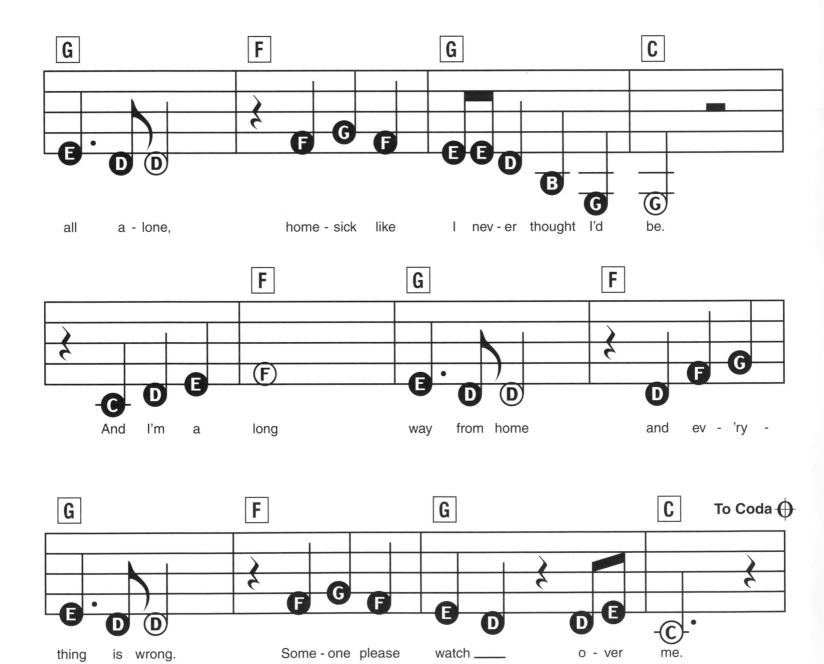

I'm a long way from home and so all a-lone, home-sick like I nev-er thought I'd be. And I'm a long way from home and ev-'ry-thing is wrong. Some-one please watch ____ o-ver me.

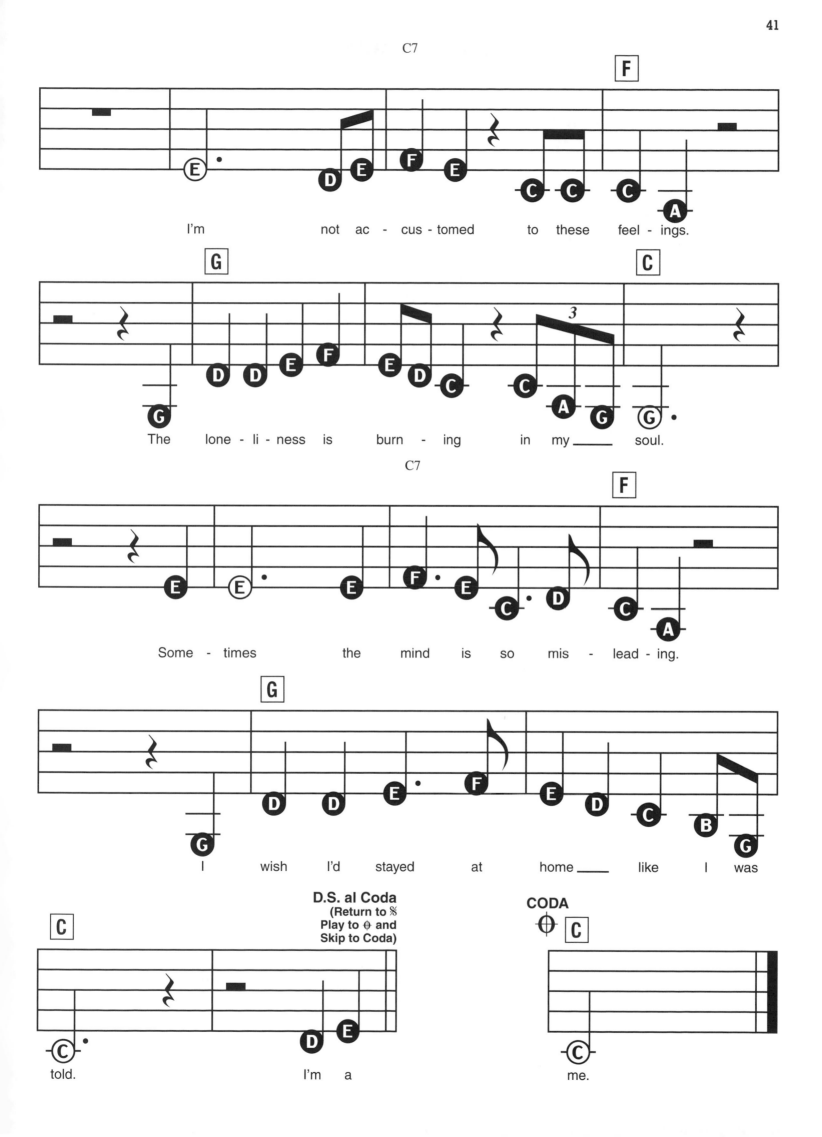

Jackson

Registration 10
Rhythm: Country or Bluegrass

Words and Music by Billy Edd Wheeler
and Jerry Leiber

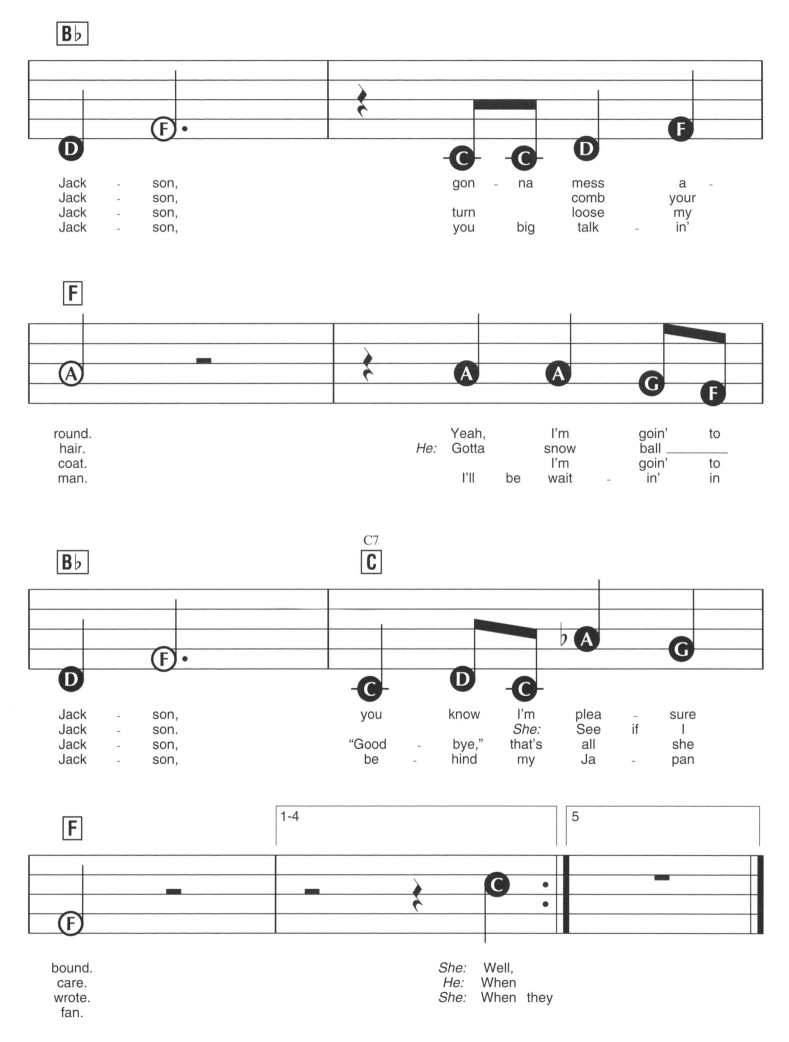

Registration Guide

- Match the Registration number on the song to the corresponding numbered category below. Select and activate an instrumental sound available on your instrument.

- Choose an automatic rhythm appropriate to the mood and style of the song. (Consult your Owner's Guide for proper operation of automatic rhythm features.)

- Adjust the tempo and volume controls to comfortable settings.

Registration

1	Mellow	Flutes, Clarinet, Oboe, Flugel Horn, Trombone, French Horn, Organ Flutes
2	Ensemble	Brass Section, Sax Section, Wind Ensemble, Full Organ, Theater Organ
3	Strings	Violin, Viola, Cello, Fiddle, String Ensemble, Pizzicato, Organ Strings
4	Guitars	Acoustic/Electric Guitars, Banjo, Mandolin, Dulcimer, Ukulele, Hawaiian Guitar
5	Mallets	Vibraphone, Marimba, Xylophone, Steel Drums, Bells, Celesta, Chimes
6	Liturgical	Pipe Organ, Hand Bells, Vocal Ensemble, Choir, Organ Flutes
7	Bright	Saxophones, Trumpet, Mute Trumpet, Synth Leads, Jazz/Gospel Organs
8	Piano	Piano, Electric Piano, Honky Tonk Piano, Harpsichord, Clavi
9	Novelty	Melodic Percussion, Wah Trumpet, Synth, Whistle, Kazoo, Perc. Organ
10	Bellows	Accordion, French Accordion, Mussette, Harmonica, Pump Organ, Bagpipes